Tough Teddies

Tough Teddies

and other bears

by Simon Bond

Clarkson N. Potter, Inc./Publishers
DISTRIBUTED BY CROWN PUBLISHERS, INC. NEW YORK

For Linda

Published by Clarkson N. Potter, Inc., One Park Avenue, New York, New York 10016

CLARKSON N. POTTER, POTTER, and colophon are trademarks of Clarkson N. Potter, Inc.

Manufactured in the United States of America

Library of Congress Cataloging in Publication Data

Bond, Simon.
  Tough teddies and other bears.

    1. Teddy bears—Caricatures and cartoons.
2. American wit and humor, Pictorial.   I. Title.

NC1429.B663A4   1985   741.5'973   85-3518
ISBN 0-517-55832-7

10 9 8 7 6 5 4 3 2 1

First Edition

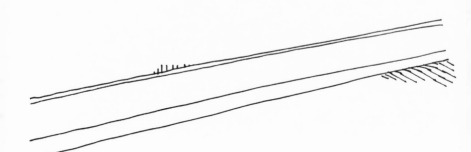

"One medium rare and one with honey."

INSECURITY HITS WALL STREET

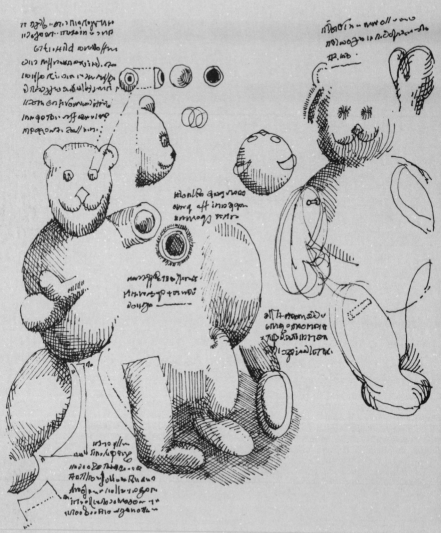

Leonardo's First Drawings

Picasso's teddy

1910

"If he can do that, I reckon he's got what it takes."

HOTEL
HEARTLESS

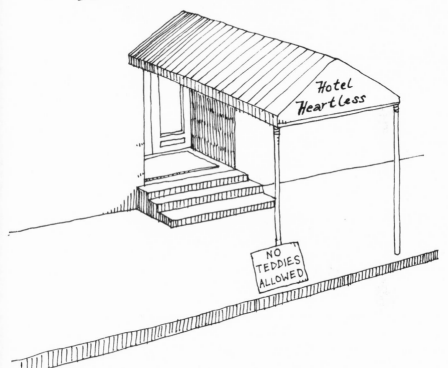

Hotel
Heartless

NO
TEDDIES
ALLOWED

BATHRO

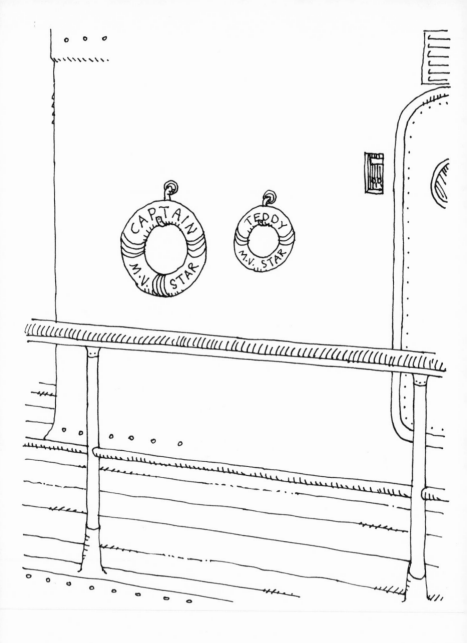

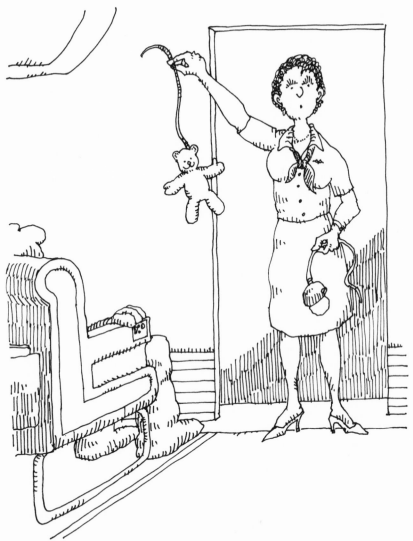

"... and in the case of continuing emergency, a teddy will drop into your lap from the compartment above."

"So you'd better start talking or the teddy takes a dive...."

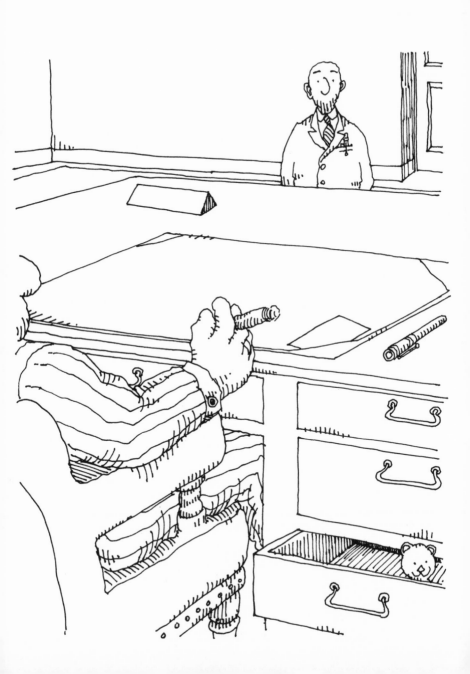

"Welcome and here are your ear and arm back."

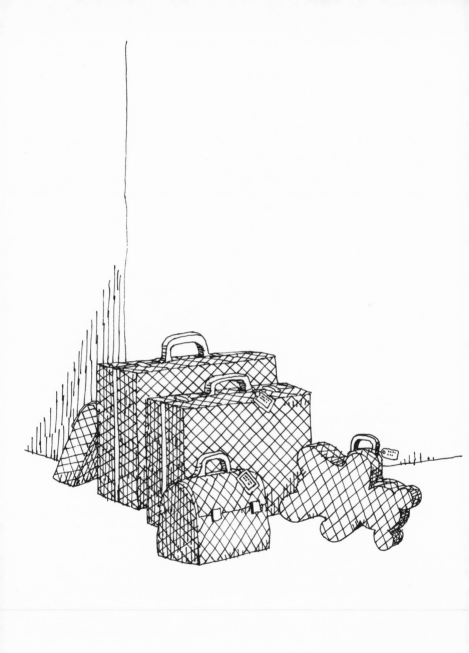

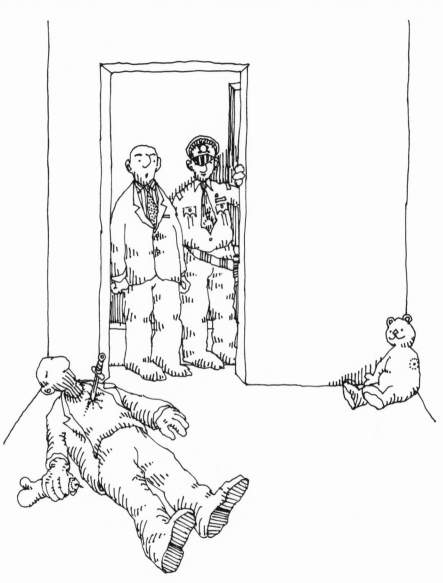

"I think we can put this one down as self-defense, Mulligan."

"...and please stop the little bastard chewing my ears."

STUPIDITY № 1

TEDDY BEARS
IN CAPTIVITY

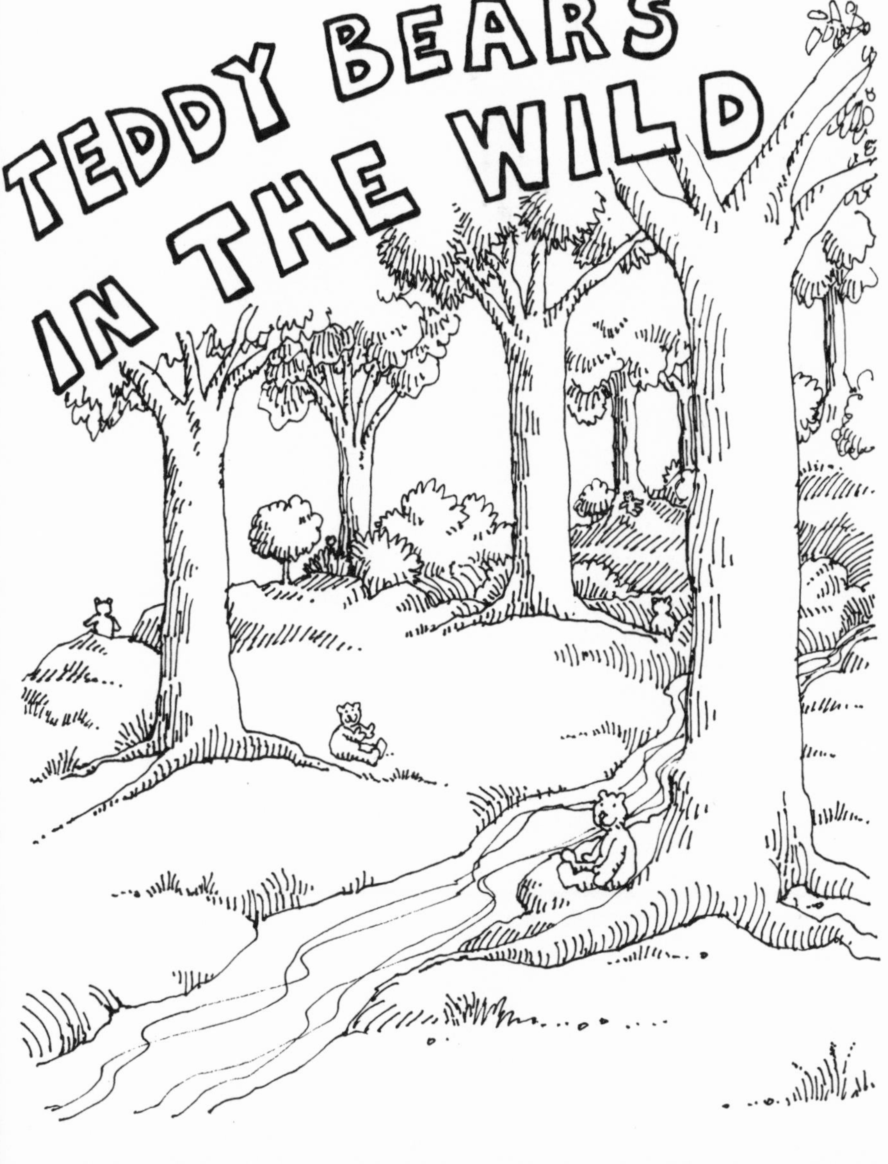
TEDDY BEARS
IN THE WILD

LONDON 1941

IN CASE OF
ANXIETY
BREAK GLASS

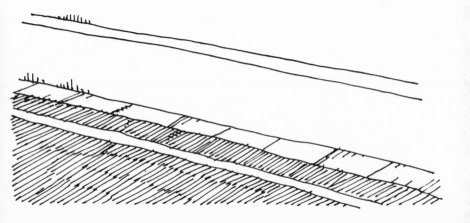

ROMULUS & REMUS
(AND THEIR BROTHER DEREK)

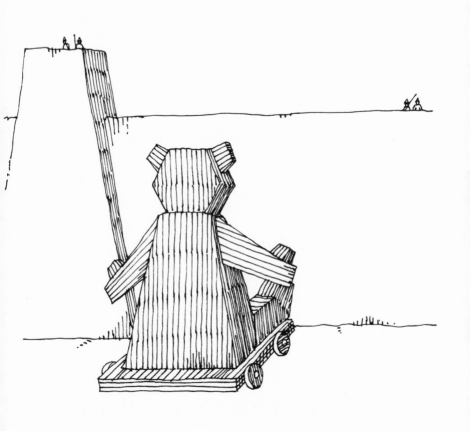

THE FIRST ATTEMPT

WERNHER VON BRAUN'S
FIRST EXPERIMENT

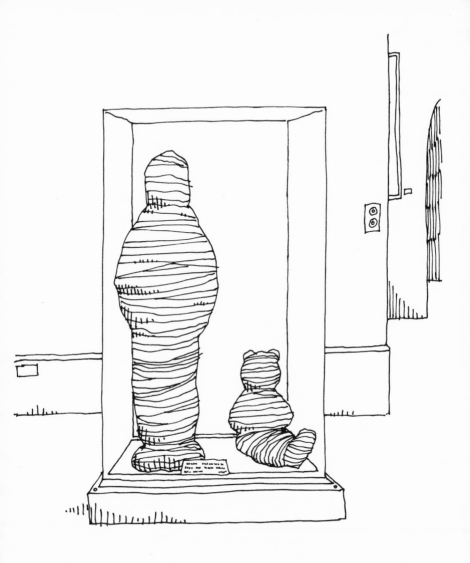

THE
SPANISH INQUISITION
STOOPS TO AN
ALL-TIME LOW

"You'll find them a very friendly tribe."

THE TEDDY TEST

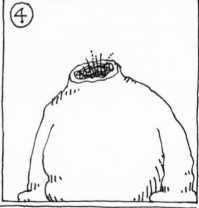

○ LORD NELSON ○ VINCENT VAN GOGH
○ CHARLES MANSON ○ RICHARD III

Match each Teddy with its very famous owner.

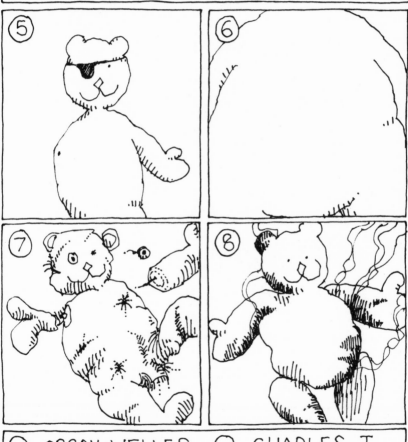

- ⑤
- ⑥
- ⑦
- ⑧

- ○ ORSON WELLES
- ○ JOAN OF ARC
- ○ CHARLES I
- ○ CYRANO DE BERGERAC

THE
3 BEARS

THE POCKET
VERSION

THE END OF INNOCENCE...

... but in the end love conquers all.

About the Author

SIMON BOND has always liked anything smaller than himself and, accordingly, is the proud owner of five teddy bears. He is hoping to acquire more in the future through either marriage or theft.